A Collection of Light

Poetry & Prose

NEEME

ISBN 978-0-646-81307-3

"Imagine", whispered my soul,
"if this pain had not happened
you might never have had anything
to write about".

MUM & DAD –

You say thank you to someone that has opened a door.

So, to you I say:

Sesquipedalian

Hwl

Thaumatrope &

Macushla.

In the hope that one day we can rearrange the letters to

form a word that describes what you actually

mean to me.

It does not exist

One does not plant a seed & then dig it up everyday

to see if it has germinated.

Give it time – it will sprout when it's ready.

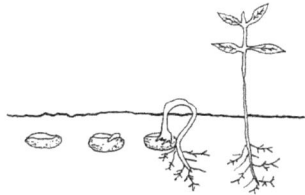

I am a thousand glorious suns &

a million transcendental sunsets.

What part of you thought you could take a bit

of me & leave the rest for later?

When you were only ever a guest in my orbit.

"Tell me a secret" I whispered to the cactus.

Against an inky sky, with the moon over her shoulder

she burst into bloom.

"Not everyone is made for the light".

Sometimes the smallest things create the biggest
changes;
Or have you never heard the first bird
of the morning reminding the earth to wake up and spin?

I am a boat on my own river,

sailing on tides of intention,

weaving past monsters from my own depths

that try to grab my oars.

My name is not easy,

It does not roll off the tongue.

It's as if my mother upon giving birth to me said;

"Let every introduction be a challenge

so that when real problems arise she remembers

all the times she won".

I don't make decisions easily.

I toss & turn & tumble down paths & possibilities.

That I've decided on you so quickly is only because

I saw stars collide behind your eyes;

And that, my love, is a once in five hundred

lifetimes event.

stellar collisions.

The foetus stretched out in the fuzzy darkness.

The old man stretched out for his daughter's hand.

"We have everything we've ever asked for" they chanted.

"What more is there for me in any place but this?".

Next

And I realised, that just like the sun,

you were oblivious to how many paths you had lit

& how many people you had helped grow.

Is that your destiny?

Where do I begin and where do I end?

This fleshy machinery whirrs & spins

& yet I still wonder where the control room is that

I call home.

I forgot for a time that magic hummed beneath my skin.

That I am more luminescent than a new-born star.

So, if you see me whirling at dusk in the rain of a crescent moon thunderstorm do not fear.

It's just that I had forgotten, for a time, how to dance with life & I never wish to forget again.

rainbows are just water that
remembered

on the darkest of days
to let the light in.

A bushfire

is chaos to all

but the eucalypts

who simply see it

as a chance to flower again

& grow.

Things the bush taught me.

What is more beautiful than a freckle,

that was born under the harshest conditions,

to remind you that there is so much in you

worth saving?

The winter snow will melt when it's ready.

The summer heat will ebb away.

Autumn's leaves will make way for the cold precisely when
they need to.

And springs flowers will bloom under no command
but their own.

So, yes, my love, you will move on too
& the timing will be nothing short of perfect.

Long after the embers of the words that you uttered
have been smothered and faded into nothingness
they will remember that you made them feel loved.

I had to remind myself to be patient

because I had danced with dreams for so long

that I felt you tug at me

long before you even knew you held my thread.

the great wait.

DO NOT BE AFRAID OF THE DARKNESS.

IT IS JUST AN ILLUSION

LIKE ME.

LIKE YOU.

Teach your heart to speak in vulnerabilities,

let it become fluent in risk & joy.

There are many shades of brave

but none as freeing as the heart that says;

'I think I'll try again'.

the language of the soul.

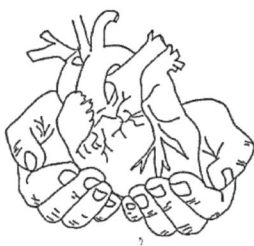

And she welcomed death as an old friend because
she had decided early on that chances were like
butterflies – suddenly emerging, beautiful & then gone
& she would catch every single one.

You ask me why & I say because the wind cannot be caged.

You ask me why & I explain that watching a storm roll in

from the ocean is beautiful in its chaos

but only from a distance

I don't trust you with my heart.

My hope for you is that at least once in your life

you find yourself at a crossroad between surety

& a leap of faith.

And love, I pray, that if only once,

you look up to the stars,

breathe in that terrifyingly beautiful moment,

smile ……..

& remember to jump.

get busy living or get busy dying.

Beware of those summer clouds that drift into your

life on a soft breeze.

One is just a pretty form

& the other a fleeting feeling —

both of which lack substance.

I prefer rain.

Have you ever seen a bird tug on the ocean

stirring her into turmoil;

or be seen by a thousand eyes

in many places at exactly the same time?

I haven't either but my, can that bird sing.

I was lead,

You were light,

A patient minute,

A match of might.

Perspective.

New friends are good but old friends
have rented out rooms in your heart,
the messiest ones scattering themselves
in corners that you most often find on
rainy days.

He asked you to be small, not so that you would not be big,

but so that you could both be small together.

You said, "a hurricane slows for no man"

& continued to be a tempest.

I am absolutely certain that my heart speaks a foreign tongue.

After all these years, right when I think I know what it's saying,

it will pull me so violently towards a person or path

that I would never have considered, that I now know

what it feels like to be a foreigner in my own home.

the hearts tourist.

What is the quickest way for happiness

to die?

To be jealous that the poppy next to you is taller,

more colourful & in a larger field, all the while

forgetting that you are a ladybug.

comparison

No, I am not a lady & I will not close my legs.

I will leave them open so that you remember

I am a creator of worlds,

A destroyer of antiquated beliefs,

A genie who never had cuffs.

So that the women before me who broke that lamp

can melt it down & use it to rappel into this world

to marvel in delight at how far we've come.

So, no. I am not a lady & I will not close my legs.

Tug me here, push me there.

Knead me into a shape that can fit under your skin.

Let me find a home there.

I want to know all of your darkness,

I want to kiss it on the forehead & hold both of its hands.

What good is it if I only see your light?

Every page of you is important not just the final chapter.

There is a trick to life I think.
& most of it revolves around
how much you loved.

And maybe, right now all you can remember

are those tales about loss.

So, let me remind you of the story of dandelion flowers

& summer rain clouds & acorn trees;

Which, perhaps, aren't stories at all, but are beautiful things

that have known loss too & found that without

losing there would be no way to grow.

There is this thing that you dream of so much;

you can taste it on your tongue & caress it at night.

So, what if I said you might have all of it in a year

or most of it right now?

So much of life is based on our decisions.

Choose wisely my love.

Might is a risk but most feels a lot like

settling.

DUSKLIGHT

The earth screeched so loudly when the first tree fell

that the men's bones rattled in their sockets

& shook the axes to the ground;

And as one they turned and walked away.

"How can we kill something so very much alive?"

they said.

Your mother is a warzone.

Your father a country she used to call home.

You've bent yourself over,

limb after limb,

contorted yourself into an overpass.

But we all know the saying about bridges.

How often they get burned.

Casualty.

There you are, the road that runs next to mine.

Never quite meeting

but glimpsed through intersections as friends pass through.

parallel soul mates.

They say that death has no fans;

but I have been your biggest advocate twice now.

On the first time we met you were ten years too late

& I wondered if I should have cheered a little louder.

On the second you were ten minutes early &

I wondered if the banner had been too much.

to the minds that can fly in the bodies that have forgotten.

And there you go again,

rejecting something beautiful because you cannot

accept the beauty in yourself.

You are to me like light to the bud of a flower.

You barely have to look my way

& I can feel my legs parting.

It's not that I didn't have the words,

It's that I had too many;

& they always came tumbling out all at once,

so that I drowned in a tangled mess

of letters & syllables.

When I saw you at the pub.

I've seen you before, you who claw & rake at me.

I've known you by name, I've rasped it out.

You who wish to take down resistance‐

the feelers, the game changers, the dream shakers.

Try to make them believe that they are mad when all along

they were free.

to the free minds, alternative thinkers & social non‐conformists.

Different is beautiful.

"I saw the ocean hold hands with the river today" said the sun.

"They laughed & giggled & wove into one.

Even you, Moon, have the Earth. I see you wink

& shine down on her every night".

"There will be someone for you" said the moon wisely.

"I don't think so" said the sun closing her eyes.

The comet was excited. She had been waiting a long time

to see the Sun again.

But when she came close the Sun had her eyes closed.

The comet turned around unperturbed.

"I will wait a little longer for her" she whispered to the Moon.

"It is not every day you find someone that makes you burn a little

brighter".

SOMETIMES IT IS THE WORDS
THAT GET MISSED THAT CAUSE
THE MOST

Today I found a light. It kicked me in the ribs
like a foetus in slumber & lit me alight from the
inside out.

hope, something I had forgotten.

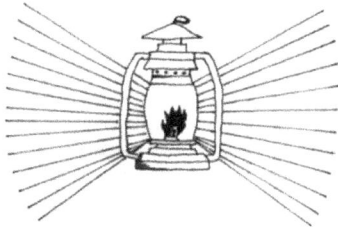

In the brown eyes of strangers

& the jumbled letters that rearrange into your name on a page;

In moments before sleep

& scents on the wind;

I find you everywhere I am not looking.

So, no I don't miss you.

Not in the way other people might.

I miss you the way a stargazer misses the stars during the day —

with the knowledge that you haven't really gone

& I will see you again if only I wait long enough.

for dreams of the endless night.

When the cloud broke & the summer rain fell,

the people threw their hands up in relief

& danced in the street.

And the cloud smiled at the people that loved her rain,

knowing they would never know that it took her

months to steal each drop.

The end result

What makes you think you can capture my attention?

I am restless to my core.

In the last 5 seconds I've travelled between realms;

watched flowers make love;

found universes within worlds

& worlds within days.

If you want to know me, magic better call you by name.

(*to the people that have called me arrogant or aloof*),

sorry, it's just that I wasn't really there.

There is a part of you in every inch of me.

I don't know when I left the door open,

but you trod lightly & etched your name into every corner;

So much so that if I took a cell from my finger

& asked to whom do you belong?

It would say to you,

to you.

Stop looking for shade from their light & for torches in
their darkness.
Duality exists to remind us that we would not
appreciate the crash of a band if we had never
found silence.

both are beautiful.

"I can't see where this path is going"

grumbled the badger as they walked through the woods.

"Doesn't that make it far more fun!" said the universe.

"Traitors" I whispered,
as my muscles & nerves
colluded without my consent
& pulled your lips to mine.

Tell me.

How many times will you wake from slumber unhappy,

with the same mindset,

on the same side of the bed,

look outside as the seasons end

& not realise that everything has changed but you?

How could I forget you?

You are like the bitumen of my youth.

Even now I hear you calling;

"I still have a piece of you".

The clouds parted to make way for the sun;

The flowers blossomed & danced with the bees;

The wind teased the waves & tickled the birds into a chorus;

But I had asked for a rainbow & so I saw & heard none of it.

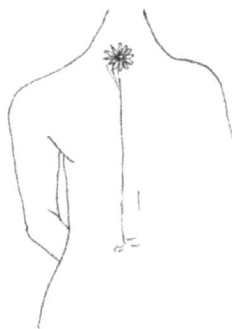

You see, the scary thing is that when I look at you, I feel
the flood of a million memories;
Flashes of warm skin on old hands & moments
when our stomachs hurt from laughing way too hard.

And oh, being with you is as easy as a heart beating.
And my, we are deliriously happy.

You see, the scary thing is that when I look at you, I feel
the flood of a million memories & also
nothing at all.

the decision.

Fall into me, into the spaces between that no one
knows about;
Where insecurities dash & dive between losses
& dreams that never eventuated.
Fall into me & tell me I was never alone.

And I have never loved a paradox as much as when

I saw your heart breath in &

felt your tongue beat arrythmia.

And with a single swing you fell the ancient

oak till it lay in two pieces on the ground.

"Don't worry", you said, "we can put it back

together & it will grow".

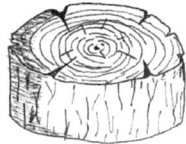

This is an ode to silent spaces —

the hush of the dawn before sunrise,

the seconds in between lightning & thunder,

the pause before the wave hits the shore,

the gap in between heart beats when your hand brushed

against mine.

can we do all four together?

Could a single sigh create a gale on the other

side of the ocean?

I'm not sure, but I sat awake in a storm last night

& between the howls

I'm sure I heard you say my name.

Doubt & regret danced side by side at their wedding.

"What a pair we are!" they exclaimed.

"Do we not complement each other perfectly?".

My soul is a fortress with a picket fence.

Don't tell me you just want to be friends &

then expect to see more than the garden.

You don't get to be upset that boundaries exist

& the windows leading to where the magic happens

are sealed shut.

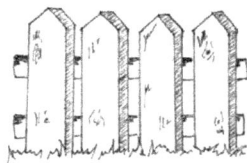

I cannot be angry at my soul,

I heard the whispers that echoed in the night

long before I cared to listen.

You do not have a final chapter,

There is no last page.

Right now, might feel like the end

but there are worlds inside you ready to be explored.

Can't you feel the universe bending to your will?

Now tell me again why you can't be loved?

IT IS THE VOICE THAT WHISPERED
WHEN I WAS THE MOST STILL;
THAT RIPPED AWAY THE LIES & TOLD ME
THE HARSHEST TRUTHS.

Silly girl,

I am not an easy option.

Do you see this in my chest?

This is an inferno.

Now watch as this burns you down whole.

The irony of time is that sometimes forever can last 7 years, while the second it took your heart to crumble & harden can remain with you for eternity.

I'm sorry that you felt you had to be small.

As if the height from your country

& the colour of your skin would cast a shadow

in which nightmares grew.

So, remember, next time you start to shrink:

mountains do not stoop to make the landscape

more comfortable.

Nor should you.

And she caged her heart and threw away the key

only to realise that metals weakness is the

persistency of water & she was in a flood.

Water always wins.

Sometimes all you need is a balm to slow

the gush of blood from your veins.

The trouble is when that balm has a heartbeat;

it is easy to forget that as one wound closes a whole

new one tears open.

wound transference.

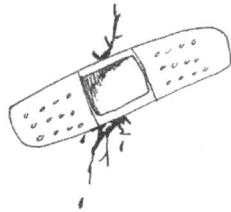

If your love cost a lifetime,
I would consider it a
bargain.

You told me that it would be an easier life

but my infinite soul balked & raged in my chest,

clawing at the walls.

"Enough", it hissed, "You did not travel through

time & space to be anything but you".

I listened & it was the bravest thing I've ever done.

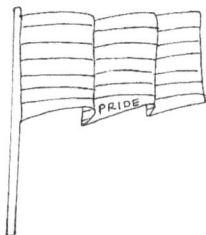

"What will I get out of this?" you asked;
And I thought, one day I hope to live in a world
where I never hear that question.

Do it because smiles nourish souls;
because the light you give makes everyone brighter;
because the tapestry you weave affects that next generation.

Do it because a single candle can ward away the dark,
but a roomful can illuminate the sky.

I cradled you in my hands & held you by my fingertips.

gently, I asked if you would nestle between my scars

& wait to see the dawn.

You were hope and last night you were the only thing

that kept me breathing.

depression

In the end there was no trumpet parade,

the sun was not eclipsed,

there was no cascade of exploding lights.

There was just a girl with her hand outstretched,

wondering where all the words we said to each other would

end up.

Would they be together, holding hands, in another place,

finishing the story we imagined.

I hope they are.

It is a sad thing to think, that after all,

they were just a string of letters

placed cleverly in the correct order

to mean everything

& also, nothing at all.

Grief is often carried twice.

First – with the help of loved ones.

Second – by yourself, as a dull ache

that can't quite be found,

because it isn't meant to hurt anymore.

Healing is not linear.

Imagine being the tear that started in your soul,

leaked from your eye,

traced your lips

& settled between your breasts.

Oh, how wonderful it would be to follow that

trajectory.

Now imagine if I was the cause of that.

What a small & fragile thing a wish is.

Yet I saw you take flight,

in the dead of the night,

on squally winds,

carrying a bundle of hope,

with wings that only knew happy endings.

every fallen eyelash is a
possibility.

You smell like ancient meetings from

times gone past and dances in the midnight rain.

You smell like hello.

Just like the sun on a snowy day, you leave me dripping.

Speak slowly. My body & soul desire it.

The former wants to hear you;

The latter wants to listen.

There's a large part of me that craves sunset drives

with no destinations;

sliding down hills on bodyboards in the midst of thunderstorms

& 3am conversations with our feet on the wall & warm wine.

Speak to me about stars & dreams

& collisions of fate.

Those are the things that make me breathe a little deeper.

I'm going to need you to dig.

Sometimes safe is good but never in love.

Save your safe for rainy days under the doona.

Safe has never taken you to the doorstep of a girl

on the other side of the ocean,

with leaden tongue and your heart in your hands

to say, "I think this belongs to you".

Our souls held hands in dreamtime

& plotted schemes for our bodies to collide;

so that when we finally met

we would become so entangled

they would never have to wait

for our eyes to flutter shut again.

We all have a little madness in us.

It is that thing that crawls under your skin itching to swim
naked under the moon

or whispers in your ear to sing at the top of your lungs down
crowded streets.

What a tremendous shame if it were to never find its way out.

After all, the best stories are always the ones with

the most amount of crazy.

If words hold vibrations let my name be thick on your tongue

so that when it finally emerges from your mouth

the friction is such that it causes your foundations

to crumble & civilisations to emerge.

I was once told that I give too much of myself too easily.

Yet it is only humans that make a game of love.

As if my soul came here to sing only half a song.

As if the sun should dim herself just to fit in.

I want to love so entirely, that long after I'm gone,

you will find me in fissures on the other side of the earth;

& when they crack me open you will understand why they say

you cannot hide the sun with one hand.

We sipped from paper cups & counted the stars,

reaching for moments so entwined with fantasy

that now when I close my eyes

I wonder if it had only been a dream.

LOVE ME LIKE THE WIND,

FIERCELY,

ALWAYS THERE,

BUT FREE – MOSTLY FREE.

And with dustpan & brush you swept

up all the parts of me that were cosmic dust

& put it in your belly.

"Grow in here" you said, & I did

& you were perfect.

It was not a lucky thing mum, I chose you on purpose.

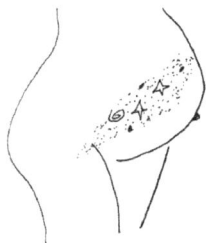

I have never been a lover of halves.

A crescent moon,

a sleepy bud slightly open from the morning sun.

So, if you find yourself looking at a shadow,

know that I am not a lover of halves —

I do not fall like the rain; I buckle like an avalanche.

there is no in between (I don't like grey).

Only death knows what will become of old friends,

who drink warm wine

& tell dirty jokes under comet trail dust.

But I have always found that they make life's

journey a little easier

& a lot more fun.

Kiss me in all the wrong
places.

the right places have

been far too greedy.

On a dusky night,

gazing at the sky with starlight in your eyes,

a firefly danced around your lips & rested on your shoulder.

"Tell me everything" I demanded as it flew back

giddy & in love.

Jealous.

You see I have grown greedy for time with you.

So much so that when you move on to the next world

I will make sure to claw my way to be first

in line for you.

One lifetime is not enough.

I hope the only things you ever surrender to

are soft kisses and clean bedsheets

still warm from drying in the midday sun.

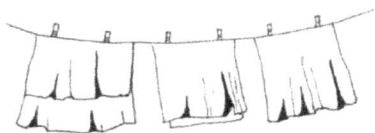

If you were a cloud & the cloud was the sky

& the sky spread forever until it was night

& the night turned to day & the day came too soon.

Maybe then you would know how much I love you.

When the sand washed to sea & got battered & turned,

when the speck got eaten & turned into a pearl.

When the man plucked the oyster & marvelled in delight.

Maybe then you would know that I'll love you tonight.

When the wind caught a smell & the smell caught a gale

& the gale it grew stronger & stronger each day.

Till the storm hit the land & petered out over the dunes.

Maybe then you would know that you should be home soon.

When the sun saw the girl & the rays hit her skin

& the freckles combined to protect what was within.

When the tan faded away & left nothing but you

maybe then you would understand what I felt like too.

My mind & heart are lovers so intimately enchanted

with flying away from the mundane that some mornings

I wonder if they regret my persistence in calling them home.

But we've only just met, you barely know me.

And how could I explain that we had met,

a million times over, in a million different ways

if only in my head.

Dreams that are forgotten are never lost
but simply curled up in slumber
in the realm between now and never
waiting for you to take their hand.

I have always been drawn to people a little bit odd

or different.

There is something in their soul that sings to mine,

in a tune that is more than familiar,

with words I think I've always known.

But perhaps that's because I'm a little different too.

and I thought, what a talent it is

to whisper loudly, without words,

in the middle of a crowded room,

from across the desert & sea.

Falling has its own vocabulary.

It's windswept nights & sweaty palms,

crowded glances & first words.

It's scraped knees & taut hamstrings

& the feeling you get before the roller coaster drops.

It's all the things I'd forgotten & thought I would

never remember.

It's you, you, you.

Perhaps when I pass into the next world

they will find the thread that connected me to you,

that pulled me in all the right directions

& weaved its way into my soul.

You are a part of me friend.

And you thumbed down my spine & leafed through the pages

but before you had read a single word you snicked it shut.

"I already know this ending" you said.

Knowing.

And I shall have a cacophony,

A bonfire,

A rave beneath my sternum or nothing at all.

I shall not sacrifice a single beat of that madness

for anything less than an explosion.

What a small & simple sentence *I love you* is.

How many other three words can

slow the push of blood in your veins

& cause endorphins to erupt

& cascade towards cells even your

body had forgotten.

I have always believed in fate.

That a tiny tug at the right second could mean

our lives become forever intertwined.

But what if my fate is to chase you

& while I'm sitting, praying for a collision,

the stars are holding their breath,

on the edge of their seats,

waiting for me to wake up, figure this out

& start to

run.

There is too much hate in the world to pass
on the request to kiss a freckled girl at sunset.
Especially if she smiles at you with the surety
that you are going to say yes anyway.

dedicated to sunset kisses everywhere.

WHEN I LOOK AT THE MOON,

I DO NOT QUERY THAT I SAW THE MOON.

SO TOO IT IS WHEN I LOOK AT YOU.

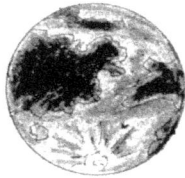

"The beauty of a star is that it's light will still reach you

even when you don't see it,

even when it's not near.

That is why they are all I write about" said the poet.

And perhaps, I thought, that is why the only thing

I ever write about is you.

There were places of endless ocean filled with
humans who had learnt how to breathe salt
& worlds where stars were so bright you could catch the rays
& contain it within jars.

Expanses of gases where dust motes glittered in your lovers
eyes caught in the reflection of an eternal bonfire.

And deserts of endless night where animals & humans
sat side by side.

"Where can I find these places?" the little girl asked.
I tapped my temple.
"Would you like to see the rest?".

From your mind crept the darkest of monsters.

Spindly & toothed.

Ravenous & horned.

But they did not scare me.

I held out my hand & took them by the claw.

Because the best of you wasn't perfect,

the best of you was flawed.

Make me afraid of how I am.

Tell me to question my own soul.

Take me to the trumpet parade of my flaws

& introduce me to the conductor.

March with me to that drum,

I've always liked a syncopated beat.

Look to the light I left on.

When the air feels like fog in your lungs – there it is.

When your skin tightens &

no longer feels like home – there it is.

When the night is not chased away by the dawn – there it is.

I would not lead you to it & deprive you of that adventure.

The journey is yours alone.

Self-growth.

There was magic in the way you said my name.

As if all four letters could be sentinels against the dark

& encompass you in warmth all at once.

And if nameless was the price I would give you all four.

Because what does a tendril of heat need with a name

when language is irrelevant between sparks.

inferno

The best words are still within me

hidden beneath my tongue.

Like an adder they will strike & sink into my flesh.

And my cells will sing;

"Necrosis! I've been waiting for that poison".

ABOUT THE AUTHOR

Neeme is a poet/writer/storyteller/musician/illustrator
from Perth, Western Australia. She loves the snow, the sun
& the impact of short poetry and prose.

She mainly writes for herself, sharing her work on social media
in between song writing and drawing. Neeme's poetry is drawn
from experience.

@neemepoetry - Instagram

www.ingramcontent.com/pod-product-compliance
Lightning Source LLC
Chambersburg PA
CBHW032039040426
42449CB00007B/948